Wales is, of course, more than just a pretty face. Gaze a little deeper again and you'll discover a distinctive sense of place, an identity that springs direct from the country's history, heritage and culture. Wales is the definitive 'Land of Castles' – there are over 400 of them, ranging from mighty medieval monuments to forgotten ruins. It's a warm-hearted country of traditions, of festivals and events which welcome everyone. Rural workshops, woollen mills and galleries are the bedrock of a thriving arts and crafts scene. Then there's the Wales of the 21 vibrancy and confidence you'll detect in places like Cardiff Bay, where one of Europe's most dynamic new waterfronts is taking shape.

This is a country of many faces, as you'll see from this pictorial journey through Wales.

The Brecon Beacons National Park.

South-West Wales

The dominant feature here is the Pembrokeshire Coast National Park, which extends around the tip of Wales for 180 miles (290km) from Amroth near Tenby to Poppit Sands, Cardigan. Along the way there's stunning scenery, one of the finest stretches of coastal natural beauty in Europe. And although it's Britain's only coastal-based national park, its boundary dips inland to include the Preseli Hills, a haunting area rich in prehistoric remains.

As befits such an unspoilt coastline, the resorts here retain a pristine period charm. Tenby, the most popular, is picture-postcard perfect, from its Georgian harbourside up into its maze of medieval streets. Solva, St Davids, Dale and Newport prove that small is beautiful – and all are perfect bases for walking the magnificent Pembrokeshire Coast Path.

There's more superb coastline along the grand sweep of sandy

1 Whitesands Bay, near St Davids in the far west of Pembrokeshire, is set amongst some of the most ruggedly beautiful coastal scenery in Britain.

Carmarthen Bay. The coast and country of Carmarthenshire inspired poet Dylan Thomas – you can visit his beloved boathouse home at Laugharne. Inland, the River Teifi winds its way through a beautiful wooded vale lined with historic market towns and villages, none prettier than Cenarth, where the ancient coracle is still used by fishermen in search of salmon and trout.

2 Strumble Head near Fishguard. It was close to here, in 1797, that Britain suffered its last invasion. But it didn't last long. The motley French force was soon seen off by the locals.

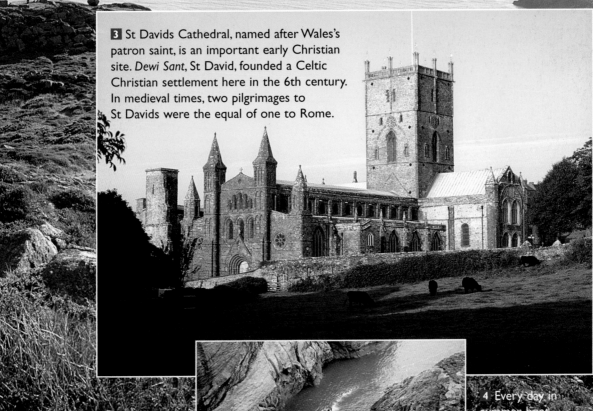

3 St Davids Cathedral, named after Wales's patron saint, is an important early Christian site. *Dewi Sant*, St David, founded a Celtic Christian settlement here in the 6th century. In medieval times, two pilgrimages to St Davids were the equal of one to Rome.

4 Every day in summer, boat expeditions from St Davids go out for exciting close-ups of the rich marine life on the Pembrokeshire coast.

5 Tenby, at the southern gateway to the lovely Pembrokeshire Coast National Park, is a seaside resort with a difference. Its perfect Georgian harbourside and narrow medieval streets give it a unique character and charm.

6 Take the boat from Tenby for the short trip to Caldey Island, home of a monastic community which produces a perfume from the island's gorse and wild flowers.

7 Solva, at the head of a long sheltered inlet, is a safe haven for sailors along Pembrokeshire's west-facing St Bride's Bay.

8 The skeletal Pentre Ifan Cromlech (a Stone-Age burial chamber) in the Preseli Hills above Newport, is made of the same Pembrokeshire 'bluestones' that it is thought were transported nearly 200 miles (322km) to Stonehenge on Salisbury Plain.

9 Carreg Cennen Castle, perched on a cliff overlooking the Black Mountain near Llandeilo. This atmospheric 'eagle's nest' is the most dramatically located medieval stronghold in Wales.

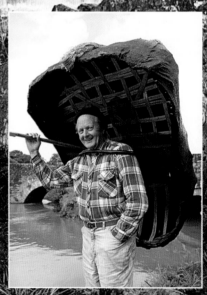

10 Dylan Thomas spent the happiest, most productive period of his life at the sleepy seatown of Laugharne on Carmarthen Bay. His much-loved boathouse home beside the 'heron-priested shore' is now a museum dedicated to his life and work.

11 The coracle, a tiny one-man fishing craft, has been used in Wales for over 2,000 years. Coracle fishing still takes place on the River Teifi, and at Cenarth there's a coracle museum.

12 The River Teifi slips and slides over rocks at Cenarth Falls, a beauty spot famous since the early days of tourism when Victorian visitors made it part of their 'Grand Tour'.

13 Handsome Carew Castle – note its beautifully carved, stone mullioned windows – is picturesquely located beside the tidal waters of the River Carew.

14 South Pembrokeshire's cliff-backed coastline at its most spectacular – the great sea arch at Stack Rocks.

15 Pembrokeshire's sea cliffs and islands are home to a prolific birdlife. Puffins (pictured), razorbills, guillemots and Manx shearwaters are just some of the many species that breed here.

16 Woollen mills throughout Wales produce weaves based on traditional Celtic patterns and motifs.

17 Here's one beach that never gets crowded. The vast sweep of sands at Rhossili on the tip of the Gower Peninsula, Britain's first official Area of Outstanding Natural Beauty.

18 North Gower's low-lying coastline is very different from that of the cliffs and headlands along the south of the peninsula. At Penclawdd, cockles are still picked by hand on the tidal sandbanks.

19 Swansea's Maritime Quarter, an award-winning redevelopment of the old docklands, has renewed the city's historic links with the sea.

South-East Wales

It's difficult to know where to begin when describing this diverse area. Cardiff, Wales's confident, cosmopolitan capital city, stands on the south coast, along with Swansea and Newport. Just to the north there are the South Wales Valleys, an area rich in both industrial heritage and unexpected natural beauty. Northwards again takes you into the wide, open spaces of the Brecon Beacons National Park, South Wales's exhilarating 'great outdoors'. Two Areas of Outstanding Natural Beauty complete this jumbled jigsaw – the Gower Peninsula and the Wye valley on the English border.

Cardiff is a stylish city, where the grand neo-classical civic architecture rubs shoulders with a bold 21st-century waterfront. Swansea's modern Maritime

20 Chepstow Castle looks out across the mouth of the River Wye to England. It is an important landmark in more ways than one: dating from just after the Norman Conquest, it is reputedly the first stone-built castle in Britain.

Quarter also makes the most of its coastal location – in this case on sandy Swansea Bay, which leads to the untouched beaches and cliffs of Gower. It's all just a stone's throw from the Valleys, the powerhouse of the Industrial Revolution. The hills are now green again, though compelling reminders of the past still remain at places like the World Heritage Site of Blaenavon, home to Big Pit Mining Museum. The grassy flanks of the Brecon Beacons are irresistible to walkers, pony trekkers and mountain bikers. This green, refreshing high country sweeps across South-East Wales for 519 square miles (1,344sq km). And at the gateway to Wales the River Wye runs through a lovely, wooded valley between the towns of Monmouth and Chepstow.

21 The graceful ruins of Tintern Abbey, a Cistercian monastery founded in 1131. The abbey is set in the wooded Wye valley, a designated Area of Outstanding Natural Beauty. This scene has inspired many famous writers and artists, including William Wordsworth and J.M.W. Turner.

23 A striking addition to Cardiff's skyline – the state-of-the-art Millennium Stadium, a major new sports and entertainments arena, stands right in the heart of the city. It has taken over from the legendary Arms Park as Wales's shrine to rugby.

22 The smoking room at Cardiff Castle. Ornate and gilded additions were made to the medieval castle in the 19th century by the fabulously wealthy Marquess of Bute.

24 Cardiff's own White House. The city's neo-classical Civic Centre, fronted by the domed City Hall, has drawn comparisons with the civic architecture of Washington DC and New Delhi.

25 Were these, the first all-weather shopping precincts, a precursor to the modern mall? Canopied Victorian and Edwardian arcades, lined with speciality shops, are enchanting features of Cardiff's thriving city centre.

26 The National Museum and Gallery at Cardiff concerns itself not just with Welsh matters. It also contains a world-class collection of art and sculpture that includes many modern masterpieces.

27 The Cardiff of the 21st century is emerging along Cardiff Bay, where one of Europe's most ambitious waterfront developments is transforming the rough-and-ready 'Tiger Bay' of old into a fashionable new part of the city.

29 Caerphilly Castle, the 'sleeping giant'. Only recently has Caerphilly's stature as one of Europe's finest surviving medieval strongholds become more widely appreciated. Its massive stone and water fortifications are a formidable example of the concentric 'ring-within-ring' system of defences.

28 The Wales of bygone times comes to life at the Museum of Welsh Life, St Fagans, on the outskirts of Cardiff. Historic buildings – including farmhouses, a chapel, schoolroom and workers' cottages – from all over Wales have been re-erected in beautiful parklands.

30 A typical Valleys scene. Tightly packed terraced houses cling to the hillside at Stanleytown in the Rhondda valley, where 'King Coal' once reigned supreme.

31 The narrow-gauge Brecon Mountain Railway runs into the foothills of the Brecon Beacons from its terminus just north of Merthyr Tydfil.

32 A succession of mountain ranges soars and dips across the horizon within the Brecon Beacons National Park, a 519-square-mile (1,344-sq-km) expanse that stretches from the Welsh border almost all the way to Swansea.

33 The distinctive flat-topped summit of Pen y fan, at 2,907 feet (886m) the highest peak in South Wales. The mountain's open, ice-sculpted slopes rise above Brecon to form the heart of the Brecon Beacons National Park.

34 Until 1980, Big Pit at Blaenavon was a working coal mine. Today, it is Wales's National Mining Museum where visitors can take a tour underground guided by ex-miners. Blaenavon's important mining and ironmaking past is recognized by its status as a World Heritage Site.

ROSE OF BRECON

35 Pleasure craft now use the 35-mile (56-km) Monmouthshire and Brecon Canal, which travels through some of the loveliest countryside in the Brecon Beacons. The canal was originally used to transport limestone, coal and wool.

36 Hay-on-Wye is the internationally famous 'town of books'. At the last count, there were around 30 bookshops in this small border town (including the castle and old cinema), selling everything from antiquarian tomes to pile-'em-high bargains.

37 The ruins of Llanthony Priory, locked away in the Vale of Ewyas. Little has changed in this undisturbed spot, deep in the Black Mountains, since the times when a medieval chronicler described it as a place 'truly calculated for religion'.

38 The fortified Monnow Bridge – a rare medieval survivor – still guards the western entrance to the historic town of Monmouth.

39 The Tudor manor house of Llancaiach Fawr near Nelson in the South Wales Valleys is a piece of living history. It convincingly recreates a day in the life of the house during the Civil War period.

40 Caerleon, or *Isca*, was one of the Romans' most important bases in Britain. Amongst its wealth of Roman remains is a well-preserved amphitheatre, built to seat 5,000 spectators. On somewhat more shaky ground historically speaking, the amphitheatre is said to be the legendary Round Table of King Arthur.

41 The National Showcaves Centre for Wales at Dan-yr-Ogof, Abercraf, is Europe's largest showcaves complex. Visitors can explore a labyrinthine system of passageways and chambers, created by the action of water on limestone rock.

Mid Wales

The unexplored, unhurried heartlands of Wales are to be found here, in the wild Cambrian Mountains, amongst gentle border country and along the graceful Cardigan Bay coastline.

It's a beguiling area where the pace of life is still dictated by the seasons and farming traditions. Travel westwards from the borders and you'll notice subtle differences with each mile. The

landscape starts off in typical border fashion, an undulating skyline of rounded hills and hidden valleys dotted with black-and-white half-timbered dwellings. But before long

42 Llangrannog on Cardigan Bay. From the beach there is a spectacular walk to the headland of Ynys Lochtyn, which spears into the sea from the Iron Age hillfort of Pen Dinas Lochdyn.

43 The Victorian resort and university town of Aberystwyth, midway along Cardigan Bay, is the unofficial 'capital' of Mid Wales. Constitution Hill, above the seafront, can be ascended by an electric cliff railway of 1896 vintage.

the mountains begin to take hold as you climb into the heights of the Cambrians – the remote 'backbone of Wales' – where sturdy, stone-built farmsteads are the preferred style of abode.

The red kite epitomizes the essence of this part of Wales. This rare bird of prey has re-established itself here, so much so that central Wales is becoming known as 'Kite Country'. It is also Wales's very own 'Lake District', which includes the scenic Elan Valley reservoirs and dramatic, mountain-ringed Lake Vyrnwy.

Countryside meets coastline along Cardigan Bay, the great horseshoe-shaped arc that stretches from Cardigan all the way to Snowdonia. Along its length you'll find charming little seaports, resorts, sailing centres, two outstandingly beautiful estuaries – and even, perhaps, spot a dolphin or two swimming in its waters.

44 The pretty sailing centre of Aberdyfi at the mouth of the River Dovey. It is associated with *The Bells of Aberdovey*, a well-known song inspired by the legend of a city lost beneath the waves.

45 When the Victorians built reservoirs, they did so in style. The Craig-goch dam is one of four in the Elan Valley, constructed to supply Birmingham with water. Dressed stone and decorative design give the reservoirs a presence lacking at most modern civil engineering projects.

46 From rudimentary beginnings in the 1970s in an abandoned slate quarry north of Machynlleth, the Centre for Alternative Technology has grown into an agenda-setting 'village of the future' which employs a host of ingenious energy-saving devices.

47 Spot the difference. The judging at the Royal Welsh Show, held each summer at Builth Wells, is taken very seriously. But the show doesn't just attract farmers. This colourful countryside jamboree has all kinds of entertainments that appeal to a wide audience.

48 Pony trekking is popular throughout Wales – these riders are exploring the foothill of Cader Idris, near Dolgellau. Centres offer the visitor everything from a few hours in the saddle to inclusive weekly holidays.

49 Barmouth's picturesque harbour at the mouth of the Mawddach estuary. The headland above, known as Dinas Oleu, is an important conservation landmark – in 1895 it was the first piece of land to be acquired by The National Trust.

50 Mountains meet the sea in a most seductive manner along the Mawddach estuary in the southern reaches of the Snowdonia National Park.

51 It's difficult to believe that stately Powis Castle, Welshpool, began life as a humble border fortification. Over the centuries it evolved into a treasure-filled mansion. The splendour is not confined just to the castle, for Powis – now in the care of The National Trust – is surrounded by magnificent grounds and Italianate terraces.

52 Offa's Dyke, the great earthen barrier constructed in the 8th century, marks the first official border between England and Wales. Sections of the dyke still survive, especially in the timeless, forgotten hills around Knighton. The long-distance Offa's Dyke Path is popular with walkers.

53 Aberaeron's Georgian-style harbour is an architectural gem. The port was built to a strict plan by 'old mad clergyman' Alban Thomas and his wife in the 19th century.

54 The green, rolling hills of southern Snowdonia are smoother and more rounded than the rugged, rocky terrain in the north of the national park.

55 Mountain-backed Llyn Tegid, or Bala Lake, is Wales's largest natural stretch of water. The 4-mile (6.5-km) long lake is a thriving watersports venue.

56 A route to remember, with 360-degree panoramic views. You'll have trouble keeping your eyes on the road when you drive into the mountains from Machynlleth on the way to Dylife.

57 The Talyllyn Railway, running on a 7-mile (11-km) scenic route from Tywyn, is one of Wales's 'Great Little Trains'. It has an enviable reliability record – opened in 1865, it has run continuously ever since.

58 Lake Vyrnwy, hidden deep in the mountains, has an alpine quality. Fringed by thick forests and overlooked by a Gothic water tower, the lake view is reminiscent of a Swiss or Austrian scene. The man-made lake supplies water to Liverpool.

59 From its lofty crag, Harlech Castle still maintains its stern gaze over Snowdonia and the sea. The castle's original sea-cliff setting was even more impressive – over the centuries the waters of Tremadog Bay have receded, leaving it marooned high and dry.

60 The Precipice Walk above Dolgellau is aptly named. The footpath clings to a steep-sided valley, giving fabulous views of Cader Idris and the Mawddach estuary.

61 The rare red kite has made a comeback in the peaceful hills of central Wales. If you don't manage to spot the real thing take a look at this sculpture at Llanwrtyd Wells.

62 Pistyll Rhaeadr is Wales's highest waterfall. It plunges 240 feet (73m) down wooded cliffs in the foothills of the Berwyn Mountains.

63 Don't get lost. Pay attention to the map – and signposts – when driving in the unexplored Berwyn Mountains and maze of country lanes around Llanarmon Dyffryn Ceiriog.

North Wales

Pride of place must go to Snowdon, the summit that gives its name to the Snowdonia National Park. But, as with South Wales, the north's boundaries encompass great scenic variety. The 845-square-mile (2,186-sq-km) Snowdonia National Park, for example, is not all mountain.

Although dominated by high and mighty peaks like Snowdon, Tryfan and the Glyders, the park also contains valleys cloaked in ancient oak woods, rushing rivers and scenic lakes.

Mountains sweep down to the sea along the sandy North Wales coast. Its string of popular seaside resorts have a perennial appeal – none more so than Llandudno's immaculate seafront, complete with a Victorian pier which maintains a rare charm and integrity. The same can be said for the Isle of Anglesey and Llŷn Peninsula, two Areas of Outstanding Natural Beauty on

64 Stone walls and green farmlands rising to rugged high country – a typical Snowdonia scene.

the strength of their exceptional coastal scenery.

In the north-east there's another Area of Outstanding Natural Beauty, the Clwydian Range, which rises above the verdant Vale of Clwyd. The views from this lofty range of hills are seemingly endless, extending from the Cheshire Plain in the east to the heather-covered Denbigh Moors and distant Snowdonia in the west.

65 This classic Snowdonia rockface will be etched in the memory of all self-respecting climbers – the triangular profile of Tryfan along the Nant Ffrancon Pass.

66 Snowdon and its neighbouring peaks, from the waters of Llynnau Mymbyr. At 3,560 feet (1,085m), Snowdon is the highest mountain in England and Wales. The Welsh name for the area is *Eryri*, meaning 'Haunt of the Eagles'. The peak itself is known as *Yr Wyddfa*, 'The Burial Place'.

67 Mountaineering the easy way. Take a 4¹/₂-mile (7-km) ride from Llanberis – weather permitting – on the rack-and-pinion Snowdon Mountain Railway right to the top.

68 Sunset over Snowdonia. This collection of challenging peaks, over 3,000 feet (900m) in height, has been a magnet for outdoor enthusiasts since the birth of climbing in Britain. The team that first conquered Everest trained in this jagged, fractured landscape.

69 Visitors can take a spellbinding underground tour at the Llechwedd Slate Caverns, Blaenau Ffestiniog, the former 'slate capital' of North Wales.

70 Dancers and musicians from all over the world come to Llangollen each summer for its colourful International Musical Eisteddfod, first held in 1947 'to help heal the wounds of war'.

71 Skilled hands can split blocks of slate into wafer-thin measures. Slate-splitting demonstrations take place at the Llechwedd Slate Caverns.

CROESO
WELCOME
LLANGOLLEN
Lle mae Cymru'n Croesawu'r Byd
Where Wales Welcomes the World

72 The tumbling cataract at Swallow Falls near Betws-y-Coed, one of North Wales's most famous beauty spots.

73 Portmeirion is … beguiling, dazzling, unique, surreal, eccentric, other-worldly. Words fail to capture the visual bravura of this architectural extravaganza, created by Sir Clough Williams-Ellis between the 1920s and 70s.

74 Take your pick – on the beach or in the water. Abersoch doubles up as both a popular seaside resort and sailing centre

75 Porthdinllaen, on Llŷn's northern shores, is the perfect coastal village. Long may it remain so. Thankfully, its future is assured, for it is now owned by The National Trust.

76 The Vale of Ffestiniog Railway, which operates on a 13½-mile (22-km) narrow-gauge track between Porthmadog and Blaenau Ffestiniog, was originally built to carry slate.

77 Possibly the most famous of them all. In a 'Land of Castles' Caernarfon lays claim to top spot. It was built by Edward I in the late 13th century to serve as a royal palace as well as seat of military power. Together with its sister castles at Beaumaris, Conwy and Harlech, it is a World Heritage Site.

78 Even by Welsh standards, Criccieth's headland castle has witnessed an eventful history. It endured more than its fair share of action in the troubled medieval period, when it was captured and recaptured by Welsh and English forces.

79 The sheltered harbour of Amlwch in Anglesey wasn't always this peaceful. In the 18th century it was a hive of activity when it served the massive copper mine at nearby Parys Mountain.

80 The vast beach at Newborough on Anglesey's south-western shores has wonderful views across to Snowdonia and the Llŷn Peninsula.

81 South Stack Lighthouse on Holy Island was built to warn shipping of the treacherous cliffs at the approach to Holyhead harbour. The coast here is renowned for its seabird colonies.

82 Plas Newydd, on the shores of the Menai Strait, is a splendid 18th-century mansion set in magnificent grounds. The house and gardens are now in the care of The National Trust.

83 Beaumaris, at the eastern entrance to the Menai Strait, is an elegant little seatown. Its name derives from the French *beau marais*, meaning 'fair marsh'.

84 Take a deep breath and say: Llanfairpwllgwyngyllgogerychwyrndrobwllllantysiliogogogoch. And what does the world's longest place name mean? St Mary's [Church] by the white aspen over the whirlpool, and St Tysilio's [Church] by the red cave'.

85 The beautiful, boundless beach at Red Wharf Bay on the eastern shores of Anglesey.

86 For the best view of Llandudno's stylish seafront take the Cabin Lift to the top of the Great Orme headland.

87 Llandudno's Victorian pier. This charming period piece epitomizes the way in which Llandudno has avoided the excesses that have blighted so much of Britain's seaside.

88 In a town full of historic houses, Conwy's Plas Mawr ('The Great Hall') is undoubtedly the most impressive. Dating from the 16th century, it is regarded as the finest Elizabethan town house in Britain.

90 The National Trust's Penrhyn Castle, on the outskirts of Bangor, is an awesome sight. If anything, it is more impressive inside than out – its cavernous Grand Hall has to be seen to be believed. It was built for that purpose – unashamedly to impress – by an immensely wealthy local slate magnate. As such, it is an extreme embodiment of the no-holds-barred Victorian spirit.

91 Chirk Castle, a National Trust property, is a home as well as historic monument. Unusually, it has been continuously lived in since it was built as a border stronghold in medieval times.

92 Erddig near Wrexham is another of The National Trust's splendid Welsh houses. It's more than a standard stately home, for it offers a rare glimpse into the 'downstairs' as well as 'upstairs' life on a country estate.

93 The Laburnum Arch at The National Trust's Bodnant Garden in the Vale of Conwy. The garden's most celebrated feature is at its best in late May and early June.

94 Beddgelert is one of the most picturesque mountain villages in Snowdonia. Its beauty is such that you wonder why, a few centuries ago, the locals invented the heart-rending legend of the faithful dog Gelert to put it on the map.

95 You know you're in Wales when you arrive at the lovely Vale of Llangollen, a mountain-backed gateway which suddenly springs from the flat Cheshire Plain.

96 The 'eyes of Ruthin'. These Dutch-style dormer windows are just one of the many treasures to be found in this architecturally outstanding little town.

97 Views far and wide from the airy Clwydian Range above the Vale of Clwyd, a designated Area of Outstanding Natural Beauty.